W9-BKL-711

WITHDRAWN

Slangalicious

Where We Got That Crazy Lingo

TEXT BY
**Gillian
O'Reilly**

ILLUSTRATIONS
BY **Krista
Johnson**

ANNICK PRESS

TORONTO + NEW YORK + VANCOUVER

Annick Press Ltd.

We acknowledge the support of the Canada Council for the Arts, the Ontario Arts Council, and the Government of Canada through the Book Publishing Industry Development Program (BPIDP) for our publishing activities.

Editing by Barbara Pulling
Copy editing by Elizabeth McLean
Cover design and interior design by Irvin Cheung/iCheung Design

The text was typeset in Sabon, Corporate, and Knobcheese
The art in this book was rendered in Gouache

Cataloging in Publication

O'Reilly, Gillian
     Slangalicious : where we got that crazy lingo / by Gillian
O'Reilly ; illustrated by Krista Johnson.

Includes bibliographical references and index.
ISBN 1-55037-765-5 (bound).—ISBN 1-55037-764-7 (pbk.)

     1. English language—Slang—Juvenile literature. 2. English
language—Etymology—Juvenile literature. I. Johnson, Krista (Kristjana Johnson) II. Title.

PE3711.O74 2004   j427   C2004-901581-8

Printed and bound in China

Published in the U.S.A. by	**Distributed in Canada by**	**Distributed in the U.S.A. by**
Annick Press (U.S.) Ltd.	Firefly Books Ltd.	Firefly Books (U.S.) Inc.
	66 Leek Crescent	P.O. Box 1338
	Richmond Hill, ON	Ellicott Station
	L4B 1H1	Buffalo, NY 14205

Visit our website at: www.annickpress.com

Contents

For Alan and Ian

"Dad, Mom, puh-leeze,"
I exclaimed.

Chapter 1

A Web of Slang

They stopped talking— for a few minutes, at least.

Don't get me wrong. My parents are okay, but they both have their offices at home. This means that when I come home from school worried about a project the teacher just assigned, they both are right there. With advice. Lots of advice.

We were in the kitchen; I'd thrown my knapsack on the floor and plunked myself down at the table, where my parents were having a tea break. When I told them I had to do a project on slang, my dad said, "That could be a really interesting topic. You know, there's slang in the music world, and slang from different types of work, and I bet you could find lots in sports. I remember when we were kids..."

And then my mom said, "You know, countries develop their own slang words. The same word can have a completely different meaning from one country to another. And there's rhyming slang, too. Of course, it's hard to track down the origins of some words, but didn't I see something in the paper the other day about..."

That's when I cut in. I reminded them, "It's my project and I'll find out what I have to by myself. Anyway, what is there to eat? I'm starving!" (I'm always starving.)

I put off thinking about my slang project for a couple of days—who wouldn't? But then I figured my parents would start getting on my case, and I remembered that the teacher wanted to see rough notes for our projects by the middle of next week. So I got a dictionary and a thesaurus from my parents' bookshelves, and before dinner, I sat down at the desk in the study. (That's the name my parents give to the room where they put their old computer and where my brother and I are expected to do homework away from the TV and other "distractions.") There I was with the books on one side of my desk and the computer humming away on the other. The dictionary was open to the page with "slang," but all it said was:

> **slang** (origin unknown) 1. Language that is regarded as very informal or much below standard educated level. 2. The special vocabulary and usage of a particular period, profession, social group, etc.

On the computer screen, a search engine was telling me that there were about 795,000 sites relating to slang and that the search had taken only 0.15 seconds. I figured it was going to take me a little longer than that to do my project. Especially if no one knew where the word "slang" came from in the first place.

Now maybe my eyes were getting tired, or maybe too much homework was scrambling my brain, but suddenly I thought I saw two little people walking across my computer screen. "Uh oh, some new virus—my parents will freak," I said out loud.

"Freak out"

Freak out

From the 1960s, freak out meant to have a bad experience with drugs; by the 1980s, to lose control. The "out" has been dropped in recent years.

"Freak," said one of the little people, a guy who had pieces of paper sticking out of every pocket. "That's a slang word."

"Exactly," added the second little person, who was dressed in clothes like the ones I'd seen in photos of my great-grandmother when she was young.

This was definitely getting weird. "What are you talking about, and what are you doing in my computer?" I whispered so Mom and Dad wouldn't hear.

"We're here to help you with your homework problem," said the man. "Think of us as slang experts."

"But who are you? And why," I asked the dressed-up person, "are you dressed like someone from a long time ago?"

"You want to know our names, our *monikers,* our *handles?"* she responded.

"I'm Edmund," the man interrupted. "And Lexie here is dressed like a *flapper."*

"Flapper with jelly bean"

"Flapper," recited Lexie. "An independent young woman from the 1920s who wore skimpy skirts, cut her hair short, danced all the new dances and used all kinds of slang words that were new and modern. Like 'Pipe the snaky socks on that jelly bean.'"

"That means 'Look at the snazzy socks on her boyfriend,'" explained Edmund.

I laughed at all these nutty words. This slang business might turn out to be fun after all. In fact, my curiosity was making me forget how strange the whole situation was. "Where did a crazy word like flapper come from?" I asked.

Boyfriends

Flappers' boyfriends were called *jelly beans, flippers* (opposite of flappers), *goofs, jazzbos,* or *sheiks.* The last term came from the 1921 movie *The Sheik,* which starred Rudolph Valentino, the Leonardo DiCaprio of his day. A young man who took his flapper for a ride in a car or bus was a *cuddle cootie.*

"Some people think it came from a word for teenage girls from forty years earlier," answered Edmund. "Some people point out that it was an old word for a young duck and by 1910 was used to refer to independent women, especially those campaigning for women's right to vote. But, really, no one knows."

"That happens with slang words," added Lexie. "People use slang in conversation for a long time before the expressions get written down. By the time someone writes them down, everybody has forgotten how they started."

"Great," I moaned. "Now I have a project where no one knows how *anything* got started."

"Don't sweat it," said Lexie.

"That's a 1960s expression. It sounds strange coming from someone dressed like a flapper," commented Edmund with a little frown.

"Oh, Ed, slang is meant to be fun," retorted Lexie. "Why say 'lots' when you can have *oodles?* Why use 'excellent' when *copacetic* or *the bee's knees* sounds more exciting?" She turned to me. "Now about that project: we're here to help. We've got our own special Web site. Let's get to work."

"Bee's knees"

"Well," I thought, settling back in my chair, "this is certainly a new way of doing a project. I could get to like it."

The Big Picture

...Slangalic

"Wait a minute!" I jumped to my feet. I had suddenly remembered that anyone going by could hear me talking to the computer. I tiptoed to the door, stuck my head out to make sure my parents and brother were out of earshot, and then closed the door quietly but firmly. Back in my chair, I nodded to Edmund and Lexie and said, "Here's my first question. Have people always used slang?"

"Probably," said Edmund. "Ancient Greek writers used it over 2,000 years ago. Shakespeare put slang in his plays in the 1500s. The first English dictionary of slang was put together by one Francis Grosse about 220 years ago in 1785."

"It was called, let me guess, *The First Dictionary of Slang*."

"No, it was called *A Classical Dictionary of the Vulgar Tongue*. The word 'slang' was used then only to describe the special language of tramps and thieves. It wasn't used to describe what we think of as slang until about 30 years later. By then it could also be employed as a verb meaning to use slang or abusive language."

Edmund paused to adjust his glasses. "Now, where does the word 'slang' come from?" he went on. "There is a theory that the term might come from an old Norwegian word meaning throw, the same word that 'sling' comes from, but no one is sure."

Roman slang

You can find slang in the comedies that Greek and Roman citizens watched thousands of years ago, but Roman slang influenced modern languages, too. The French and Italian words for head *(tête* or *testa)* come from *testa*, the Latin word for clay pot. A tough Roman kid might say to another Roman kid, "Get out of here or I'll knock your clay pot off."

"Testa"

"You mean this 'origin unknown' stuff again?" I sighed. Edmund obviously liked explaining the history of words, but his answers didn't seem to be all that helpful.

"Yes, but let's look at some of the ways we *do* know that slang words get created," he replied.

And with that, he and Lexie scrolled down the search engine page and pointed to one site. All of a sudden, we were on a page labeled "Slangalicious."

"This is the site where Ed and I hang out," said Lexie, "and it's a gas." While Edmund had been giving me a history lesson, her flapper clothes had changed to bellbottoms and beads, and she now looked like a hippie. "It's the most, it's something else, it's groovy."

Before Lexie could come up with more adjectives, I started reading at the top of the screen.

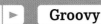

Groovy

While the word *groovy* became popular among hippies in the 1960s, it was being used by jazz musicians in the late 1930s and early 1940s.

Slang can be made by shortening a word, lengthening a word, borrowing a word from another language, or using the name of a person or a place.

People slang: A *brodie,* in the late 1800s, meant a leap (after a man who claimed to have jumped off the Brooklyn Bridge), then later a mistake. By the 1950s, the word was used to mean a skidding U-turn. Circus people still use it to mean a fall, with the implication that the fall was caused by stupidity or clumsiness. The word *ameche* for telephone came into being after the actor Don Ameche played the telephone inventor in the 1939 movie *The Story of Alexander Graham Bell.* The first *smart aleck* was thought to be Alec Hoag, a famous thief of the 1840s.

Place-name slang: The word *bunk* or *bunkum,* meaning nonsense, comes from Buncombe, a place in North Carolina. The representative for Buncombe once made a useless speech in an important debate, only because he felt he was expected to say something. So talk that makes no sense — that is just a lot of hot air — was called Buncombe, then bunkum and then bunk.

"Just a lot of hot air"

Slang is also made by playfully twisting language—making words that can be difficult for an outsider to decode. For instance, some slang is created by reversing the order of the letters in a word or by replacing a word with a rhyming substitute.

Backslang: Backslang is created by reversing the letters of a real word, as in the British expression *yob,* which first meant a boy, but later came to mean an uncouth, vulgar youth or hooligan. There is very little backslang in North American speech; it is more common in British speech.

Rhyming slang: Found in many parts of the English-speaking world, rhyming slang is created by substituting a rhyming word or phrase for the actual word being referred to. For example, *apples and pears* is Cockney rhyming slang for stairs. Often just the first word (*apples*) is used.

I stopped reading and looked at Lexie and Edmund, who were standing at the side of the screen. "You mean it's rhyming slang, but the words don't even rhyme any more?"

"That's right," said Lexie. "It's almost like a puzzle."

"Okay," I answered, "but that is definitely weird."

"*Okay*—now that is an interesting word," Edmund responded. "For years, people had all sorts of theories about where it came from. Then, in 1941, a professor called Allen Read became famous as 'the okay man' for uncovering the first recorded use of this slang

"Okay"

word. Here is what he found out. In the late 1830s, teenagers and college students had a fashion of misspelling words deliberately."

"That's like my older brother," I said. "It drives my parents crazy."

"Exactly. They used short forms: *N.S.* for 'nuff said,' *O.W.* for 'oll wright.' It is rather like the short forms people use in e-mail, like *btw* for 'by the way' or *lol* for 'laughing out loud.' Newspapers started imitating them for fun. On March 23, 1839, the *Boston Morning Post* used *O.K.* for 'all correct' or rather 'oll korrect.'"

"So that was the first time anyone used *okay*?"

"It was the first time anyone wrote it down," answered Edmund.

"But who thinks up the words?" I persisted.

"Read on," said Lexie, pointing to another paragraph on the screen.

Slang happens whenever people get together, so some observers see slang as a product of urban life—whether it arose in ancient market towns, at medieval crossroads, or in the huge metropolises of the Industrial Revolution and the 20th century. Slang also happens when people of different backgrounds meet. In English, you can find slang words that come from many languages, including Yiddish, Italian, Arabic, Hindi, Romany, and West African languages like Mandingo and Temne. Slang develops to describe new inventions, new situations, and new places. It spreads as people travel in their own country or in other countries. It also spreads through entertainment: songs, movies, radio, comic strips, and television.

Occasionally a word that has been deliberately made up will stick. *Beatnik* is a famous example; we know exactly who first used it and when. It was coined on April 2, 1958, by Herb Caen, a San

The Beat Generation

The Beat Generation was a term made up by writer Jack Kerouac to describe the worn-out, weary feeling of his 1950s contemporaries and their rebellion against conventional values. It drew on the long-established sense of *beat* as a slang word for exhausted and also on the jazz musicians' use of beat to mean tired or lacking in spirit.

Francisco journalist, to describe a group of *hipsters* or kids from *The Beat Generation.* This was shortly after the first Sputnik satellite had been launched by the Soviet Union, signaling the start of the space race, and Caen later said that the word had "just popped out."

The word *gobbledygook,* meaning "pretentious nonsense," was coined during World War II by Maury Maverick, chairman of the Smaller War Plants Committee in the U.S. Congress, when he complained that bureaucratic language reminded him of turkeys gobbling.

Slang also originates with particular groups of people. It can start as the special jargon of a certain profession or people in a certain type of work. It then spreads into more general use. Many slang words have originated in sports, music, or other leisure activities. Other slang words have come from the criminal world, where people want to develop a secret language to prevent the authorities from finding out what they are doing. Sometimes we can trace a slang word back to its origins, but often it has what etymologists and lexicographers describe as "uncertain etymology."

"Uncertain ety-what?" I asked.

"It means we can't be sure of the history of the word," responded Edmund, "although we can make some guesses. For instance, a *rubberneck* or a *rubbernecker* means a sightseer or tourist. Obviously, that comes from

"Gobbledygook"

English slang words

English slang words from other languages include *schlep* (to haul), from the Yiddish word for drag; *boondocks* (an isolated or wild region), from the Tagalog word for mountains; and *shiv* (a knife), from the Romany word for a blade. The word *plonk,* for cheap wine probably traveled from World War I France with English-speaking soldiers who mispronounced the term *vin blanc* (white wine). *Glitch* (a snag or malfunction), traveled from the German word for slip and the Yiddish word for slide into computer language and then into common speech.

"Rubbernecking"

the picture of people swiveling their heads around as they gaze at the wonders of the big city. On the other hand, it is hard to figure out the origin of the phrase *to put the kibosh* on something. It means to stop it, put an end to it."

"You mean like, 'My mom put the kibosh on my brother's plan to lie around all summer'?"

"That's right," answered Edmund. "There are many theories about that expression. One is that it came from an Irish word for

Etymologists

Etymologists study the formation and development of a word and its meanings. They look at the history of a word. Lexicographers write or compile dictionaries.

the cap a judge wore when he pronounced a death sentence. But no one really knows."

"Well, if we can't figure out where all the words come from, do we know *why* people use slang?" I asked.

"Because it makes language fun!" exclaimed Lexie. "For instance…"

"We've decided to go out for pizza," called my mom. "Come on down."

I jumped. I'd been so absorbed in slang I'd almost forgotten where I was, and I certainly didn't want my mom climbing the stairs to hurry me up. "Coming," I called. "Just let me finish one thing."

I turned back to Edmund and Lexie. "For instance what?" I demanded.

"Go have your pizza. We'll continue our discussion after supper. There's so much to show you," said Edmund, with a wave of his hand at the screen behind him.

"We've got the skinny on slang for you," added Lexie. "Later."

With that, the two of them strolled off the screen. I stared at the computer for a moment, then shut it off and hurried downstairs.

Thumbs
Up

Even though we ate at my favorite pizza

place (I had olives, mushrooms, and hot peppers), I kept wondering all through dinner and on the drive home—about Edmund and Lexie, about that Slangalicious site, about whether they would be there when I got back. I walked into the house, grabbed an apple, and hurried off to the study, hearing my mother say to my dad, "That much interest in homework? What's got into the kid?"

I turned on the computer anxiously and waited for what seemed like minutes instead of seconds, but then there they were. Lexie was dressed normally this time.

"Hey there," said Edmund.

"Back for more?" asked Lexie.

"You bet," I said. "You were saying that slang made language fun."

"You're darn tootin' it does," Lexie began. "Often a slang word seems like the perfect word to describe someone or something. It's appealing because it provides a shorthand description of something. A newspaper editor looking for a short, snappy headline would rather write 'Straphangers stranded as drivers hit the bricks' than 'Because of a busdrivers' strike, commuters are wondering how to get to work.'"

Lexie went on. "Also, slang is always developing, so it makes people who use it feel up-to-date and in the know, part of a select group that is hip, cool, savvy."

"However," Edmund interjected, scrolling down the computer screen, "not everyone has the same opinion about slang. Look at this."

Stix Nix Hix Pix

Perhaps the most famous use of slang in a headline was *Variety* magazine's shorthand description of the poor reception given by rural audiences to cornball movie comedies: "Stix Nix Hix Pix."

"Slang is language which takes off its coat, spits on its hands and goes to work."

—Carl Sandburg, American poet

Slang is "the one stream of poetry which is constantly flowing."

—G.K. Chesterton, British author

Savvy

Savvy is derived from a mispronunciation of the Spanish words *sabe usted*, meaning "you know."

Some people think slang is a good thing. It gives us new words that make a language richer and more colorful. It adds lively images to make what we are saying more interesting.

But there have always been people who regard slang as sloppy, trendy, and inappropriate for educated or well-spoken people to use. Jonathan Swift, whose book *Gulliver's Travels* was published in 1726, was also a minister. He complained about other ministers using slang in their sermons. He didn't like new and vulgar words like *mob* (from Latin *mobile vulgus,* "the excitable crowd") or *phizz* (short for physiognomy, a method of reading a person's face to determine character).

"Poor old Swift," Lexie jumped in, interrupting my reading. "What would he say if he knew that one of the words he made up has become a slang expression? Ever heard of a *yahoo?*"

"Yeah," I said. "It's what my dad calls people when he thinks they are rude."

"Well, Yahoo was the name Swift gave to the imaginary race of brutish creatures with a human appearance in *Gulliver's Travels*," Lexie explained. "Now it means a boorish, crass, or stupid person.

"The one stream of poetry which is constantly flowing"

So even someone who disapproves of slang can create a slang word. Keep on reading. You'll see how some slang words have become everyday parts of speech."

Some slang words become permanent and "respectable" words over time, gaining the status of what dictionary compilers call standard English; others remain slightly "unrespectable" for years or even centuries. The mob that Swift disliked so much is now a normal word for a crowd (often an unruly one), although phiz (now with one z) has stayed around only as British slang for face.

Getting down to brass tacks is now standard English for getting to the heart of the matter. Few people realize that it was once rhyming slang for facts. A politician speaking seriously to a foreign representative might say, "Mr. Ambassador, let's get down to brass tacks."

"Getting down to brass tacks"

On the other hand, *booze* (from the Dutch word meaning to drink to excess) has been used to mean alcoholic drink for centuries and has kept its slang character. You would never say, "Ms. Ambassador, what kind of booze can I get you?"

Because of its association with the language of criminals and with informal conversation, slang has often been seen as the coarse speech of the lower classes—not suitable for educated people. This attitude is evident in a passage from *Anne of Avonlea* by L.M. Montgomery, set around 1900. Anne, still in her teens, is teaching at a one-room schoolhouse to earn money for university. Here she is reproving little Davy Keith for lying:

"If you ever catch me telling a whopper again you can..." Davy groped mentally for a suitable penance... "you can skin me alive, Anne."

"Don't say 'whopper,' Davy... say 'falsehood,'" said the schoolma'am.

"Why?" queried Davy, settling comfortably down and looking up with a tear-stained, investigating face. "Why ain't whopper as good as falsehood? I want to know. It's just as big a word."

"It's slang; and it's wrong for little boys to use slang."

"There's an awful lot of things it's wrong to do," said Davy with a sigh.

In recent times, as life has become less formal and language more relaxed, slang has shed its unsavory image. However, in 2002, when a leaked e-mail showed that CNN was considering adding hip-hop slang to its newscasts to attract more young viewers, the idea was quickly criticized. News, it seemed, was not the place for slang, and CNN dropped the idea.

Hip-hop CNN

"There's so much information here," I said. "I have to put together some rough notes for the teacher and have them ready by the middle of next week. What have I got so far?"

I opened up my word processing program on the computer.

To my surprise, Edmund and Lexie appeared there too, just at the edge of the screen. I started typing up some notes. I put in the parts about how slang can be made and how long it's been around, and the part about "uncertain etymology." (Edmund had to spell that for me.) I added the part about slang being frowned on by some people.

You could say that Lexie was reading over my shoulder if she hadn't been standing at the edge of my computer screen. I guess she was reading over my cursor.

"You forgot the part about slang being used in certain jobs and then getting borrowed for use by people in general. Remember it was in your dictionary definition?"

"But we haven't even talked about that yet," I objected.

"Then we'll have a swell time looking at that topic when we meet again," answered Lexie. "Right now, it's time for some shut-eye. You should hit the pit, too."

I glanced at my watch reluctantly. "I guess so," I said, adding, "You'll be here when I start working again?"

"You can count on it," said Edmund. "Good night."

"You bet," added Lexie. "See you in dreamland."

Chapter 4

Nibbles, Nosh, and Bun Pups

It was Sunday before I got back to work on my project, and I turned on the computer with a mixture of curiosity (would they be back?), doubt (how *could* they be back?), and anxiety (what would I do if they *weren't?*). I began by opening up my rough notes.

"Let's get cracking," said Lexie, appearing on the screen wearing a chef's hat and apron. "We're going to look at slang in certain types of work."

Edmund had on a bow tie and white cap. "There are a number of professions that have given us interesting slang," he considered. "And we thought we would start with diners. Everybody likes food."

"Sure thing," I agreed.

"Our site has the best in the lingo of diners, hash houses, and grease joints," said Lexie.

"Uh, why is Edmund dressed in a bow tie and a white hat?" I asked, noticing that he looked a little awkward. I guess he didn't like dressing up as much as Lexie did.

"He's dressed as a soda jerk," said Lexie.

"That's not a nice thing to say!" I exclaimed.

"A soda jerk," Edmund informed me, as Lexie brought up the Slangalicious site and started scrolling down the page, "was someone who worked at a soda fountain—a sort of ice-cream parlor. The term came from the use of *jerk* to mean to pump beer or soda from a tap."

"How did jerk go from that meaning to the one we use now?" I asked.

"We'll get to that answer in a while," Edmund said. "First, I think we should sample some food terms."

Joint

Joint was a word with wide application. It began in criminal slang by meaning a meeting place, then spread to more general slang to mean an establishment for eating and drinking, often a disreputable one. Various words were added to define what kind of place: *gin joint, burger joint, clip joint* (a place where you were likely to get swindled or *clipped*), a *juke joint* (a cheap bar or tavern with a jukebox), or a *grease joint* (the cookhouse for circus and carnival workers).

"Joint"

"Hmm. What kind of slang can you use for meals?" I wondered.

"Haven't you ever said *O.J.* for orange juice? Or asked for eggs *over easy?*" demanded Lexie.

"Sure, but that's not slang, is it?"

Edmund nodded. "Some of the most colorful slang there is comes from the diners and lunch counters that were the modern eating establishments of the early 1900s. In soda fountains and greasy spoons, waiters and short-order cooks developed new expressions, probably to liven up the tedium of pouring endless cups of coffee or cooking up the same menu items over and over. But slang was also useful for keeping information from the customers or the owner. For instance, *thirteen*, the unlucky number, meant 'the boss just walked in.'"

"Okay," I said. "If a waitress got tired of saying hot dog, what would she say instead?"

"She might say *bowwow, bun pup,* or *groundhog,*" answered Edmund. "She'd give you a glass of *Adam's ale* or *city juice* instead of water. Three of something was called *a crowd.*"

"Hmm, 'a crowd of bun pups' sounds more fun than 'three hot dogs,'" I mused as I started to read what was on the screen.

"City juice"

Diner Slang

Some of the words created by waiters (also known as *biscuit shooters* or *soup jockeys*) and short-order cooks (*hash slingers* or *biscuit rollers*) are still widely in use, such as *BLT* (bacon, lettuce, and tomato sandwich) or *sunny side up* (eggs fried on one side only). Other traditional phrases, such as *Gentleman will take a chance* for an order of hash—a dish made from whatever was left over in the kitchen—have become less common, probably because they seemed a little too gruesome for an eating establishment.

Some diner slang plays on an image conjured up by the food (like *birdseed* for cereal) or draws on Biblical references (the Bible was an important literary source for people in the early 1900s). Here are a few more examples.

Adam and Eve on a raft: two poached eggs on toast

Axle grease or Skid grease: butter

Baby, Moo juice, Sweet Alice, or Cow juice: milk

Bowl of red: an order of chili

Burn one: put a hamburger on the grill

Burn the British: a toasted English muffin

Clean up the kitchen: hash or hamburger

Cowboy: a western omelet or sandwich

Cow feed: a salad

Dog biscuit: cracker

First lady: spareribs. This was a pun relating to Eve, the first woman mentioned in the Bible, who is described as being made from one of Adam's ribs.

Gravel train: sugar bowl

High and dry: a plain sandwich without butter, mayonnaise, or lettuce

Houseboat: a banana split

In the alley: serve as a side dish

Lumber: a toothpick

Natural: 7-Up (because 5 and 2 are a natural 7 in the game of craps)

Noah's boy: a slice of ham (because Ham was Noah's second son)

On the hoof: meat done rare

On wheels, or Go for a walk: an order to be packed and taken out

Pittsburgh: toast or something burning, so-called because of the smokestacks in Pittsburgh

Put out the lights and cry: liver and onions (*lights* is an old word for organ meats like liver.)

Stack: a stack of pancakes

Wreck 'em: Scramble the eggs.

"Moo juice"

Coffee

Coffee has attracted lots of slang terms over the years. Popular ones have included *java* (from Java, the Indonesian island that was once the prime producer of arabica coffee beans) and *joe*. (There are no reliable explanations for joe, which was first recorded in writing in 1930. However, U.S. Navy folklore claims that it was coined when Josephus "Joe" Daniels, secretary of the navy under President Woodrow Wilson, banned alcohol on board ship and left sailors with nothing stronger to drink than coffee.) Less complimentary names are *mud* and *omurk*.

In diner slang, a waitress might say *draw one* for one cup of coffee or *pair of drawers* for two. If you order a black coffee, it comes *with no cow*. An order of coffee and doughnuts is *sinkers and suds* (from the image of dunking the doughnut in the hot drink).

In the 18th century, when coffee was a new drink, one slang word for it was *ninny broth*. The implication was that "real men" drank ale or other alcoholic drinks.

"Java"

Hot Diggety: The Story of a Dog

In the late 19th century, *hot dog* began as an expression among university students for someone who was particularly good at something. The word first appeared in print in 1896. By the 1920s, hot dog was also used to mean good or excellent. A kid might say "Hot dog" or "Hot diggety" on learning that there was ice cream for supper. At the same time, hot dog became popular as a term for showy. This use can still be found in sports, where a player might be criticized for *hotdogging* or showing off.

But what about the food? Frankfurter sausages had been called *dog sausages* by American German immigrants as early as the 1860s.

So, eventually, were small sausages such as wienerwurst (sausages from Vienna, whose name was eventually shortened to wiener). The term dog sausages was probably a bit of grim humor, referring to an 1843 New York scandal involving dog-meat. British sailors in World War II gave sausages the nickname *barkers*.

"Dog sausages"

In the late 1890s, Coney Island was the favorite amusement park for New Yorkers to visit, and sausages on a bun became the visitors' favorite food. These were often called *Coneys* or *Coney Islands*. The first written record of the term hot dog is dated to 1900. In 1913, the Coney Island Chamber of Commerce tried to ban the name, because its members didn't like the idea of associating the sausages with dogs.

The word hot dog finally got respectable in 1939, when Britain's King George VI and Queen Elizabeth visited North America. As guests of U.S. President Franklin D. Roosevelt, they sampled these sausages on buns. Once hot dogs were respectable enough for royalty, the Coney Island Chamber of Commerce decided to celebrate the word. That same year, they staged Hot Dog Day.

Abyssinia

From the 1930s on, *Abyssinia* (the former name of Ethiopia) has been slang for "I'll be seeing you."

Just then I heard my parents calling me to dinner. "Gotta go," I said, "but I still have to work on these notes. Didn't you say there were more words from other kinds of work?"

"Of course," replied Edmund. "We'll look at some after you've eaten. See you later, alligator."

"Abyssinia," added Lexie.

"Lexie has the craziest expressions," I thought. I was grinning as I ran downstairs.

Greens, Geets, and the Daily Grind

"Ah, spuds, I love 'em," said my dad, checking out his baked potato as we sat down to an early dinner. "Now there's a slang word for you."

I was about to point out that we were having cow feed, too, but I thought better of it. No point in encouraging my parents to come up with more advice. So I just nodded and tucked in.

Toward the end of dinner, a familiar conversation arose. My brother started talking about how he needed a bigger allowance. He's always going on about it. I don't know why, because he and his friends do nothing but sit around and eat and stare at the TV screen.

"I need at least a few more bucks a week," he moaned.

"We're not made of money," said my mother. She always says that. "The new roof cost us a bundle. Maybe you could get a part-time job if you really need money. Although first I'd like to see more chores done around here."

I had been about to suggest that my brother find work as a soda jerk, although he'd have to work on the soda part. However, when I heard the word chores, I resolved to keep out of the conversation. "Time to leave before the jobs get handed out," I thought.

"May I be excused to work on my slang project?" I asked. I jumped up from the table, grabbed my dishes, paused to put them *very* neatly by the sink and dashed away to the study.

The screen saver on the computer wasn't the usual one. Instead, there was a slowly moving list of words that I recognized as slang words for work: *the daily grind, the rat race, the salt mines...*

"Very funny, you guys," I said as the screen saver disappeared and my notes came back along with Edmund and Lexie.

"Greetings," said Edmund.

"What's tickin', chicken?" added Lexie.

"You were going to show me words from other kinds of work. But what about words for money?"

Buck

Buck was first used in the mid-1800s as a word for a dollar. The term came from a buckskin, a deer hide used in barter.

"You mean like *geets* and *bread?*" asked Lexie, as the Slangalicious site appeared on the screen.

"Geets and bread?" I repeated. "What's that?"

"Read on," she replied, pointing to a big dollar sign and clicking on it.

Moolah, Lettuce, and Rhino

It is hard to do without money and, it seems, to do without slang words for money. In 1859, a compiler of slang observed that there were over 100 words for money, or *the necessary*. Since then, people have continued to come up with new ones.

"Fish, greens, and rhino"

Some words for money refer to its color (from the green color of American money). These include *lettuce, greens, kale, green stuff,* and *cabbage.* Others refer to the fact that money seems as essential as food *(dough, bread)* or requires hard work to get *(scratch). Rhino* began to be used for money in the 17th century, possibly because money seemed as hard to come by as a rhinoceros (an animal most English-speaking people of that time would never have had the chance to see). *Moolah* first appeared in the 1930s, but its etymology is unknown. This is also the case for *plunks* (used to mean either a large sum of money or a dollar), *geets* (used from the 1920s to the 1940s), and *spondulicks* (used from the middle of the 19th century on, and possibly connected to a Greek word for a shell).

Besides words that describe money in general, there are many slang words for particular kinds of money. A Canadian one-dollar coin is a *loonie,* because it depicts a loon on its reverse side. When the Canadian Mint brought out a two-dollar coin, it naturally became a *toonie* (even though it had a polar bear on it).

Salt money

When a Roman soldier went to work, he didn't say, "I'm bringing home the bacon" or "I'm earning my daily bread." He used the slang word for his pay and said, "I'm earning my salt-money." Two thousand years later, people still earn a *salarium* (salt money), or salary.

Smackeroo and *banger* both describe a dollar (possibly because a dollar bill could be smacked down on a table). Other words for a dollar have included *fish* (used from the 1920s to the 1940s) and *ace* (the term comes from a deck of cards, as does the word *deuce* for two dollars). *Fin* or *finnif*, slang for five dollars, is derived from the Yiddish and German words for five. A *sawbuck* came to mean an American ten-dollar bill because there were two X's on the back of the bill. The X's looked like a sawhorse, also known as a sawbuck.

"Well," I said, "my brother could choose from tons of words for money if he ever started earning some. But what kind of job could he do?"

Just then, I heard my brother thumping on the study door. "Don't hog the computer. I need to use it. My stuff's important."

"Give me 10 more minutes," I yelled, then added more quietly, "Maybe he could run away from home."

"And join the circus?" suggested Lexie with a twinkle in her eye. "I don't know how he'd work out as a *First of May.*"

"A First of May?"

"It's circus slang for a new guy, a novice. It comes from the date the circus traditionally opened. Let's look at some other circus words, like *Joey, John Robinson, Annie Oakley, Hey Rube...*"

I interrupted. "Is every slang word in the circus somebody's name?"

"Not at all," replied Lexie, now dressed in tights and turning cartwheels as she spoke. "There are *kinkers, hayburners, painted ponies, stripes,* and the *midway,* too. See for yourself."

Under the Big Top

Circus clowns are called *Joeys*, after Joseph Grimaldi (1778–1837), known as the first modern clown. The area where the Joeys get ready is *clown alley*. A *charivari* is a noisy whirlwind entrance of clowns; this kind of entrance is also called *shivaree* or *chivaree.* (Coming from French but of unknown etymology, charivari has a number of meanings outside circus life, but all are connected with the idea of a hubbub.)

John Robinson is the term circus performers use to signal to each other that it is going to be a shorter show than usual. If the master of ceremonies said he had a special message for an audience member named John Robinson, the performers would know to end their act quickly. *Hey Rube* is what a circus person yells to show he needs help, probably because he is in a fight with some *townies* (local people).

FREE PASS HOLDERS

"Annie Oakley"

An *Annie Oakley* is a free pass (so-called because it was punched full of holes, as if the famous American markswoman had used it for target practice). In the theater world, a free pass has the same name. If a circus has a *straw house*, that is, a full house with every seat sold, they won't need to give out any Annie Oakleys.

The *big top* is the big circus tent in which the performance takes place. The area between the big top and the gate, the *midway*, is where you find the concession stands with games and food. As you wander through the circus you might be attracted by the *ballyhoo,* the spiel shouted in front of a sideshow to attract attention. The word has also come into general use to mean nonsense or empty praise.

Circus slang in North America differs quite a bit from the British and European circus variety. The latter uses many words drawn from Romany slang, called Parlari. However, like North American slang, part of its purpose is to let the circus people talk to each other without the *townies* understanding.

"What about those *painted ponies* and *kinkers* you talked about?" I asked Lexie.

"Hold your horses. We're coming to that," she said, as the screen moved to the next page.

"Painted ponies"

Circus people use the term *hayburners* to refer to horses and other animals that eat hay or grass. A horse trained to do fancy steps is a *high school horse,* and a *rosinback* is a horse used for bareback riding. Zebras are *painted ponies* and tigers are *stripes.* Lions and tigers as a group are called the *big cats*, and the person who works with them is a *slanger.*

A *carny* (or *carney*) is any kind of carnival worker. An experienced circus performer is a *kinker,* probably an image drawn from acrobats. The circus manager is the *gaffer.*

"I thought a gaffer was something in the movies," I said.

"That's right," answered Edmund. "The term is also used in the movie world for the chief electrician. That's an example of how a slang word can travel from one business to another."

"How about a *dog and pony show?*" Lexie interjected.

"Indeed," responded Edmund. "A dog and pony show is a rather contemptuous slang term for a very small circus. However, it has moved into general use to mean an elaborate show or a formal presentation, often for sales or public relations purposes. A *geek* was originally a sideshow performer at a circus who specialized in disgusting acts, but the word has come to mean someone eccentric, or someone who devotes too much time to his or her studies, especially to computers."

"Computer—that reminds me, I'd better finish off these rough notes," I exclaimed. "But maybe we could look at some more slang words first. Have you got any?"

"Heaps of them," Edmund answered. "Follow me." As the screen changed again, Lexie appeared in an engineer's hat and overalls.

Working on the Railroad

Much of railroad slang dates from the days when trains were the fastest, most popular, and most affordable form of transportation. A *double-header* is a train pulled by two engines. The term was first recorded in 1869. Within 20 years, it also meant two baseball games played back-to-back. The term for a train pushed or pulled by three engines, a *three-bagger,* came *from* baseball, where it means a triple, or a three-base hit.

Locomotive engines have often been called *hogs* (possibly because they are big, powerful, and need to be fed). Consequently, the words for engineer have usually involved pigs: *hogger, hoghead,* or *pig-mauler.*

The conductor was called the *brains, skipper,* or *bull head,* or sometimes *stack* (from a slang term for the caboose). Railroad detectives were *bulls* or *cinder dicks.* Track workers were *gandy dancers,* for reasons that have never been discovered.

The fireman who kept the fires going on steam engines was tagged with the name *bakehead.* A railroad employee who traveled as a non-paying passenger was called a *deadhead.* (The term is also used in the airline industry.) In the late 1800s, railroad workers noticed that loaded freight cars

"Bakehead"

sounded a different beat over the track-joints than cars that weren't carrying a load. They called the empty cars *deadbeats* because, like the deadheads, they weren't paying their way. By the beginning of the 20th century, deadbeat was being applied to people who were idlers or who failed to do their share of the work.

A Pullman car (or sleeping car) was called a *snoozer.* A refrigerator car was called a *reefer*—a term also used by truckers for refrigerated trucks. The *band wagon* was the car or train from which wages were handed out to railroad employees—a popular place. Nowadays, to *jump on the bandwagon* means to join a person, party, or cause that is very popular at the time.

Traveling slowly was the mark of a *milk train,* which picked up milk in its refrigerated cars from stops along the way. *Milk train* came to mean any really slow train, and a *milk run* is any trip with frequent stops. Very small towns were *whistle stops.* If a steam train had to pick up water for the engines without stopping for passengers or cargo, it was called *jerking a drink.* Thus a locality that was useful only for taking on water was a *jerkwater town.* Eventually, jerkwater town gave us *jerk*—a fool, a simpleton, a stupid person, or an unpleasant person.

Hoboes

Hoboes and unemployed people looking for work, before and especially during the Great Depression of the 1930s, would *ride the rods*—sneaking onto trains or sometimes even riding underneath them (a dangerous practice). For these *boxcar tourists,* a *side-door Pullman* was slang for a boxcar where they might be able to sleep if the railroad staff didn't catch them. Sometimes, they would have to nap on *Pittsburgh feathers,* that is, a load of coal. As they waited in the *jungles,* hobo encampments usually located near the railway, these drifters dreamed about someday having an easier life. The *Indian Valley Line* was a mythical railroad with good working conditions for boomers (workers who wandered from job to job). Harry McClintock, in the famous 1928 song "Big Rock Candy Mountain," talks about a hoboes' paradise of lemonade springs and jails that are made of tin. In one verse, he describes how the railroad authorities will finally treat hoboes and tramps nicely:

> "The shacks all have to tip their hats,
> And the railroad bulls are blind
> There's a lake of stew and ginger ale too
> And you can paddle all around it in a
>   big canoe
> In the Big Rock Candy Mountain."

"Milk train"

Funny, just as I finished reading about a word for a disagreeable person, my brother thumped on the door again. "Get a move on," he grumbled. "Are you going to take all night on your project?"

"I'm almost done," I called. I added a sentence on circus slang and railway slang to my notes, then printed them out.

"I'm outta here," I said quietly, in case my brother was lurking outside the door. "I've got team practice after school tomorrow, so I won't see you for a couple of days. But you'll be back, right?"

"Definitely," said Lexie. "Smell you later." She saluted as the site shut down.

The Old Ball Game, Shinny, and More

The next morning at school, I handed in my rough notes. On Wednesday, my teacher handed them back with comments. "A good start. Please give lots of examples of different kinds of words, and don't forget to explain their origins, if you can. Perhaps you could show how some slang words have changed their meanings over time. Remember, I need to see your title page next week, too. And you will be presenting your project to the class, so you need to have three questions ready to ask them."

Piece of cake

The expression a *piece of cake* originates in the 1930s. It is similar to the earlier expressions *applesauce* and a *cakewalk* in its meaning of something easily accomplished.

Hmm, this project wasn't going to be a piece of cake.

I tried to stop thinking about slang over the next few days, but I kept coming across it. My friends and I were playing house league baseball one afternoon and a member of our team got *beaned*—at least that's what the coach said when the pitcher accidentally hit the kid in the head with the ball. At the end of the game, the coaches from both teams got us together to sing "Take Me Out to the Ball Game." (They are good coaches, but they can be pretty *corny* sometimes.)

I biked home with the song still running through my brain, wondering if *root* was a slang term, too, and where it came from. I fixed myself a snack, took it to the study, and pulled out the notes with my teacher's comments. Then I turned on the computer.

"Hi, sprout, what's growin'?" said Lexie.

"Yo," said Edmund.

"My teacher likes my rough notes but wants more examples of slang in the finished project. I've been wondering about sports terms," I said.

"Ah yes," said Edmund. "Enjoy your snack while we show you about *fungoes, rhubarb,* and *ballpark estimates.*"

"Don't forget *goons, sin bins,* and *Kitty-bar-the door.* We don't have to stick to baseball," exclaimed Lexie.

With a cry of "Play ball," from Lexie, the two of them switched me to their Slangalicious site and found the right spot. Lexie was already suited up

"Cakewalk"

Corny

Corny means sentimental, naive, banal, or old-fashioned. It probably comes from the idea that someone from the country, i.e., the cornfields, might behave in this unsophisticated manner. Other slang terms that convey a similar meaning are *schmaltzy*, which means cloyingly sweet or sentimental (from the Yiddish word for chicken fat), and *hokey*, which means artificial or sentimental and derives from the slang term *hokum*, the use of comedy or sentimentality to appeal to an unsophisticated audience.

for the game, and she was shoving a bat into Edmund's arms as I started reading.

In the Bull Pen

Whether he is a *southpaw* (lefthander) or throws right, a pitcher usually doesn't want to throw a *bean ball,* hitting the batter on the head. He might, however, try to be a *barber* and throw the ball close to the batter's jaw—offering a little *chin music.* A player who gets hit with a bean ball might get angry, charge the pitcher's mound, and start a *rhubarb.*

"Chin music"

The term rhubarb probably comes from radio theater, where background conversation was created by actors muttering "rhubarb, rhubarb." Red Barber, the famous broadcaster for the Brooklyn Dodgers, is credited with using it first, but he claimed he got it from another sportswriter, who had heard it from a third, who had heard it from a bartender.

Baseball's relief pitchers warm up in the *bull pen.* (There are several theories for the origin of this word, from the claim that pitchers used to warm up next to a sign advertising Bull Durham tobacco to the idea that pitchers were waiting to be "slaughtered.")

Fungo is an exercise where a player or coach hits grounders and fly balls to the outfielders with a special bat. We know the term dates back to the 1860s, but there are numerous theories about where the word came from. One possible source is a rhyme recited by kids playing the game; another is a Scottish word for toss.

Rooting

Whether we are talking major league or minor, *fans* (short for fanatics) always root for their team. *Root* is 19th-century slang for cheering, usually for a sports team but eventually for other individuals or groups. The word may come from *rout*, an English word for bellow, or possibly from *root*, meaning to work hard.

Another word for fan in the early part of the 20th century was *bug*. The term is no longer used for sports fans, but it survives in words like *shutterbug*, a photography enthusiast, and *goldbug*, a person who likes to invest in gold. Bug has many other slang meanings, including a germ (a flu bug), a listening device used by spies, a computer glitch, and a Volkswagen Beetle. It can also mean to annoy, and it has specialized meanings for horseracing fans, printers, and astronauts.

If a batter hits a fly that is easily caught, it's a *can of corn.* This is said to come from the days when grocers would store cans of corn on the top shelves and tip them with a stick so they tumbled down easily into their hands. But the batter might also hit a home run—*homer, dinger, long ball,* or *four-bagger*—in which case the ball is *going downtown.* If the bases are loaded, his homer is a *grand slam* (a bridge player's term for taking all the tricks in the game).

Baseball batting averages are scored out of 1.000. For example, someone whose batting average is .500 hits the ball safely half the time. *Batting a thousand* means doing exceptionally well at something or getting a perfect score (something no baseball player ever does). Someone who is tough and unrelenting is *playing hardball*. If a situation changes, it's *a whole new ball game.*

Professional ball players want to be able to play in the major leagues, *the show,* or *the big show.* This gets them out of the *bush leagues,* the minor league teams in small towns.

In the early days of baseball, if a game was rained out, spectators were issued *rainchecks* to let them return to see a later game. The first known use is 1884. Gradually, the term spread to other types of sporting events and eventually to any offer that wasn't taken up immediately. By the 1920s, it was used in England, too, probably introduced there by U.S. soldiers during the First World War.

"Just how many slang words come from baseball?" I asked.

"Well," said Lexie, looking mischievous, "we could give you a *ballpark estimate*."

"That's a term that came from looking over the stands and guessing how many people were watching the game," explained Edmund. "Nowadays, it is used to mean any rough estimate."

"Would you like to hear terms from another sport?" asked Lexie.

"How about *no holds barred?*" suggested Edmund. "That comes from wrestling and means there are no rules forbidding illegal holds. Or *dead ringer*, meaning a perfect match? It comes from *ringer*, the 19th-century word for someone who substituted for a wrestler, and *dead* as a word for absolute."

Hot stove league

When fans gather to discuss their sport, particularly in the off-season, it's called the *hot stove league*. The term, which seems to have begun in the baseball world, refers to the time between the end of the World Series in the fall and the start of the new season in the spring. However, it has spread to many other sports. *Hockey Night in Canada* even uses the term for a feature between the second and third period, in which sports journalists trade views.

"Hot stove league"

"No wrestling," I insisted. "How about a sport I like, like hockey?"

"Let's get on the ice," answered Edmund as the screen shifted.

Goons and Dekes

Since hockey is such an important part of Canadian life, it's not surprising that Canada has had a particular influence on words related to the game. *Shinny* is a uniquely Canadian hockey term. It means a *pickup* or an impromptu game played with whoever is at hand.

To deke means to fake a motion or movement so as to temporarily deceive the opposing player. Shortened from "decoy," it too is a

Canadian word, as is *chippy,* a description for a game that is rough or characterized by fights. *Goon hockey* is a violent style of hockey, featuring *goons* (people employed to terrorize opponents). The word comes from an expression for a *booby* (a simpleton or fool), but it was probably also influenced by Alice the Goon, a subhuman creature created by cartoonist E.C. Segar in his Popeye comic strip. Such a player might well find himself in the *sin bin* (penalty box) or *benched* (removed from play).

"She went high to the top shelf"

Slang words for puck include the *rubber* and the *biscuit.* A player can score a goal in any number of ways: "He *put the biscuit in the basket.*" "She *found the twine.*" "He *put the rubber between the pipes.*" "She went *high to the top shelf.*" "She went *upstairs*" (high in the net). "He went *five-hole*" (between the goalie's legs).

When a team is so far ahead in the game that all they have to do is keep up the defence, the announcers call it *Kitty-bar-the-door time* (sometimes *Katy-bar-the-door time*). Where the original phrase *Kitty-bar-the-door* came from is unknown, but its use in sports dates to 1915, when Ottawa Senators player Art Ross came up with the term to describe this very successful style of defensive hockey.

A player who scores three goals in a game gets a *hat trick.* This expression comes from cricket, where a bowler who took three wickets with successive deliveries actually received a hat. It was picked up in hockey in the early 1900s and was originally used only when a player scored three successive goals with no one else scoring in between. Nowadays, it is used more generally.

"I've heard hockey announcers talk about hat tricks," I said, "but how else is it used?"

Lexie responded. "Local politician Susan Brown scored a hat trick last night. She was elected mayor for a third term, defeating rookie candidate Scott Green. You have two slang words right there."

"*Rookie,*" explained Edmund, "originated in the 19th century and means a new recruit or novice on a sports team or in a job, particularly a military or police force. It may come from shortening the word 'recruit,' but some people think it comes from 'rook,' a word for crow, possibly because the new kid in a gang had to act as the lookout."

Loaf

Loaf first appeared in writing in 1838 as slang for hanging around doing nothing in particular. It was used by a writer named Joseph Neal, but it soon appeared in the writings of authors like Charles Dickens and Harriet Beecher Stowe. Other expressions for taking it easy have included *hack around, bean, mess around, louse around* (not from the insect, but from an English word meaning to stop working), *sluff, hang, hang out,* and *goof off.* At the University of Missouri in the 1930s, students would say, "I'm jelling." The word doesn't turn up again until teenagers started using it in the 1970s and 1980s.

"My head is spinning," I exclaimed. "There's slang *every-where*."

"Why not take a breather, kiddo?" said Lexie. "It's time to loaf, kick around."

"You mean veg, chill, put my feet up," I said. Gee, I was starting to sound like her! I liked her suggestion, too. "I got a new magazine in the mail that I want to check out. So that's it for today. See you tomorrow."

"So long," said Edmund.

"Plant you now, dig you later," added Lexie.

The Boob Tube, The Flicks, and The Funnies

When I got home after school the next day,
the kitchen was crowded. My mom was making a cup of tea,
and my brother had piled a couple of sandwiches on a plate and
was heading in the direction of the TV. "Are you going to park
yourself in front of the idiot box again?" Mom asked him.
"You'll rot your brain."

"You bet," he answered as he slouched off.

I grabbed a couple of apples and a cookie and figured it was time to head for the computer. I turned it on and settled back, thinking about how TV must be a way of spreading slang around.

"Hey, Joe, whaddya know?" said Lexie.

"How's tricks?" said Edmund.

"Hey there," I answered, then launched right in. "Let's talk about TV and slang."

"Of course," said Edmund. "In fact, why don't we start right back when home entertainment center meant a piano, with Tin Pan Alley?"

"Tinpan what?" I asked.

"The nickname for the area of New York where all the music publishers were located in the early 1900s. *Tin Pan Alley* may have referred to the cheap pianos in publishers' offices, where composers showed off their new tunes. Or it may have come from a newspaper article describing the practice of winding paper around piano strings to make a tinny sound."

"Did these publishers make records, like the ones my parents have?"

"No, they published sheet music. In those days, people bought it to perform on their own pianos or other instruments. Many of the words that were used by the Tin Pan Alley publishers later made it into regular speech: *number* for a song, *ballad* for a sentimental

The boob tube

Words for TV include the *boob tube,* the *idiot box,* the *goggle box,* the *one-eyed monster,* the *electronic babysitter,* and the *telly.* Words for TV watchers include *square eyes* and *couch potatoes.*

"Tin Pan Alley"

piece, *torch song* for a love song, and even the verb to *plug*."

"Then," added Lexie, "a new kind of music called jazz added a lot of new words to the language—words that lasted through decades. Take a gander at this information."

All that Jazz

Jazz is another word of uncertain etymology. It has been traced to several West African words—the Mandingo word *jasi* (to step out of character), the Temne word *yas* (to be energetic), and the Tshiluba word *jaja* (to cause to dance)—and to the French word *jaser* (to speed up or chatter). It may also be related to *jasm,* an earlier slang word meaning energy or drive. Wherever it came from, in the early 1900s the term started being applied to the new syncopated music from New Orleans, a city influenced by both its French and its African-American heritage. (Jazz musician Jelly Roll Morton, who had a reputation for bragging, also claimed to have invented the term jazz, but etymologists don't take his claim seriously.)

Jazz appeared in print twice in 1913—the earliest written usage. In one instance, it meant a kind of ragtime dance, and in the second, a sportswriter used it to describe a baseball team's vim, vigor, and pep. Whatever its origins, jazz was soon used not only for the music, but also to mean empty or pretentious talk and, as a verb, to speed up or liven up.

In the 1930s, the language that jazz musicians had been using became popular with the mainstream. *Swing, jitterbug, bebop, scat, boogie-woogie* (a type of music that grew out of the blues), and *jive* all

Plugging

To *plug* a song meant to promote it heavily, coming from the use of plug to mean to work hard at something. The *pluggers* who worked for music publishers would take a new song around to popular singers and try to persuade them to perform it. When the nickelodeon theaters began offering *flickers,* or silent films, the pluggers would arrange for their songs to be performed either as accompaniment to the film or as intermission entertainment.

◄ ► **Disc jockeys**

In the 1950s, as radio producers began programming more popular music for young people, the term *disc jockey* was added to the music scene. Unfortunately, so was the word *payola,* a slang term for a bribe paid to a radio station to encourage the playing of certain songs.

came into regular speech. Jive has had a number of meanings over the years, including to tease or taunt.

Cool, Hot, Hip, and Hep

Although the word *hot* had been used for decades to mean something good, it was also used to describe the improvised swing music of jazz musicians in the 1930s. *Cool,* on the other hand, came from the bebop era of the late 1930s, along with *cat* and *dig.* Like hot, cool has never left the language. A 1992 study of teen language found that almost all North American teens understand the word cool, and many have it in their daily vocabularies.

Cat was a hobo slang word for a migratory worker, but by the mid-1930s jazz musicians had adopted it to mean other musicians. In the mid-1940s and 1950s, it moved to mean a regular guy. *Dig,* meaning understand and eventually appreciate, came into use in the 1920s among African Americans. The word stayed popular through the next few decades, eventually ending up as hippie slang in the 1960s.

In spite of the hippie image of long hair, beads, and "peace and love," the term *hippie* formerly meant someone who was *hip,* as did the words *hipster* and, for a few decades, *hepcat.*

The origins of *hip* and *hep* are murky, but the most convincing explanation is that hip comes from either the word *hepi* (to open one's eyes) or the word *hipi* (to see) from the Wolof language of West Africa. For most of the 20th century, hip has meant sophisticated or aware. Hep, which had the same meaning, was fashionable for a few decades, particularly among jazz musicians.

Musicians would get together to *jam*—to play without arrangement, or to *woodshed*—work out or practice a new song in private.

(Woodshed has now come to mean practice in other fields; a lawyer might woodshed a witness she is preparing for a trial, for instance.)

Musical slang

Squeeze box, groan box: accordion
Woodpile: xylophone
Gob stick, black stick, licorice stick: clarinet
Gobble pipe: sax
Skins, hide: drums
Dog house: bass fiddle
Git box, belly fiddle: guitar
Eighty-eights: piano
Bone, slush pump: trombone

"Bone"

"It's not only music that has given us slang words," interjected Edmund. "Popular songs have been a way of spreading slang, as have movies, television, and even comic strips."

"Right, Ed," interrupted Lexie. "We should talk about movies and slang. After all, there is even a movie all *about* slang."

"You're right," responded Edmund. "And the word *movies* was once a slang term itself."

"You've gotta be kidding," I protested. "No way."

"Way!" said Edmund with a laugh. "Look here."

"No way, man"

No way, man, a phrase first recorded in the 1960s, has kept going strong with the support of movies like *Wayne's World* ("No way." "Way.") and TV characters like Bart Simpson.

Flicks and Talkies

By 1906, motion pictures had already been nicknamed *the movies.* Twenty years later, producers still considered this slang term too degrading, but the name had stuck. Other terms were the *flicks* or *flickers* (because of the way the picture flickered), *jumping tintypes* (a flapper term), and the *talkies* (a word coined when sound was added to movies in the late 1920s).

From crime and detective films to comedies, movies have popularized slang words, as well as helping to create others. (Because of his tough guy roles, legendary movie star Humphrey Bogart's last name came to mean to get something by intimidation or to take more than one's share.) In recent years, the movies *Clueless* and *Valley Girl* (along with Frank and Moon Unit Zappa's satirical song about the language of the San Fernando Valley in California) utilized *awesome, grody to the max* and *fer sure,* among other words. In *Wayne's World,* actors Mike Myers and Dana Carvey humorously recreated teen speech of the 1970s and 1980s.

Hollywood even made a movie all about slang. *In Ball of Fire,* a 1941 comedy, the glamorous showgirl and gangster's girlfriend Sugar Puss O'Shea (Barbara Stanwyck) meets shy and definitely un-hip professor Bernard Potts (Gary Cooper) when he

Duck soup

Although its origins are unknown, the term *duck soup* has been used from about 1910 to mean something easy, a pushover, or a guaranteed success. The Marx Brothers titled their 1933 film *Duck Soup.* Given the mayhem and chaos that fills the movie, it was probably not easy to make, but the brothers hoped it would be successful. It is now considered one of the greatest comedies ever made.

is investigating slang for an encyclopedia. When the police come looking for her, Sugar Puss hides out at Potts's residence, where he lives
with seven other professors, and teaches him about slang—and life.
The movie is full of expressions like "Stop beating up with the gums"
(i.e., "Stop your idle talking"), "What's buzzin', cousin?" and "Shove in
your clutch" ("Get lost").

"So watching lots of movies is good for learning about slang,"
I said. "Does that mean watching television is good for picking it
up, too? One of my favorite shows is on tonight."

"Absolutely," said Edmund. "There's nowhere near enough
time to cover all the slang that comes from TV, but here's an interesting example. *Kowabunga*, or *cowabunga*, is a word that came
directly from the early days of television, when the popular kids'
program *The Howdy Doody Show* featured a cast of characters
that included a supposed Indian chief named Thunderthud.
The actor who played the chief came up with several phrases to
express emotion, and the one he used when he was annoyed was
Kawabonga. In the 1960s, the word caught on among surfers,
who changed the spelling to 'cowabunga' and used it as an
expression of pleasure or victory. *Cowabunga* was brought
back to TV by the Teenage Mutant Ninja Turtles
and Bart Simpson. Bart has also helped to
popularize the expressions 'Been there,
done that' and 'Don't have a cow.'"

"Even some video games have
characters who use slang," added
Lexie. "But let's take a quick look
at comic strips. You'll be surprised
how much they've contributed.
Read what this says."

"Duck soup"

"I'll gladly pay you Tuesday..."

Cartoons and newspaper comic strips have also helped to spread slang widely. American cartoonist E.C. Segar was responsible for the development of several words. Segar drew the *Thimble Theatre* comic strip for newspapers from 1919 to 1938, although his strip was best known for the character he introduced in 1929: Popeye the Sailor. Along with Popeye himself, Popeye's girlfriend Olive Oyl, and Popeye's arch-enemy Bluto (later Brutus), Segar created Alice the Goon (a subhuman flunky of the Sea Hag), and J. Wellington Wimpy (famous for the phrase "I will gladly pay you Tuesday for a hamburger today"). Wimpy may have lent his name to the 1960s term *wimp* (a weak and indecisive person). The word *wimpy* has also been used for hamburger, and it is the name of a hamburger chain in Britain. Because Popeye derives his strength from spinach, his name was quickly adopted for the leafy green vegetable. A *popeye* was also the nickname given to the rear observer in a fighter or reconnaissance plane during wartime. More recently, popeye is one of the terms for a car with only one headlight shining.

Barney Google, a comic strip that has run in newspapers from 1919 to the present, was created by William de Beck. This strip contributed several new words to the language, including *yardbird* (someone confined by authority to a restricted area, for example, a prison yard or an army base), *horsefeathers* (nonsense, rubbish), and *heebie-jeebies* (nameless terrors or unpleasant fantasies, eventually used for drug withdrawal symptoms or a hangover from drinking too much alcohol).

The word *palooka,* meaning a boxer, was coined by a journalist in 1929, but it was popularized by Joe Palooka, the comic-strip boxer and gentle good guy (drawn by cartoonist Ham Fisher from 1930 to 1984). Outside of the strip, palooka has the sense of someone big but stupid.

However popular Mickey Mouse has been since his creation in 1928, the Disney character curiously came to be used unfavorably in slang. The exception is Australia, where *Mickey Mouse* has been used as rhyming slang for *grouse,* which, instead of meaning to complain, is slang for excellent.

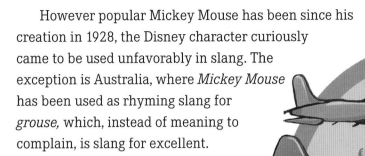

"Bomb-dropping mechanism"

From World War II came three uses of Mickey Mouse: a bomb-dropping mechanism, training films, and petty rules or red tape. The Korean War brought the phrase *Mickey Mouse* boots, rubber boots that looked like the ones Mickey Mouse wore but made the soldiers' feet sweat and consequently freeze. After WWII, Mickey Mouse also came to mean sentimental or insincere (*Mickey Mouse music*), showy or cosmetic (*Mickey Mouse changes*), shoddy or inferior (possibly from cheap watches with Mickey Mouse faces), or easy (a *Mickey Mouse course*).

"Hey guys," I said, glancing at the clock. "It's time for my show, and after that I'll go get the paper and read the comics for research. Catch you tomorrow."

"Au reservoir," said Edmund.

"See you in the funnies," added Lexie, with a wink.

Chapter 8

Slang under Fire

My mother has been working on her own project, putting together a family history. So she was looking through some pictures at the kitchen table on Sunday afternoon when I came in for a bagel with peanut butter. "Who is that with Grandad?" I asked, pointing to a picture of my grandfather when he was much younger.

"That's your great-uncle Lionel and some friends. They had just come home from the Second World War, where they had been prisoners of war after their planes were shot down. Lionel used to talk about his kriegie pals."

"Kriegie pals?"

"Yes, that's what they called themselves. It was derived from the German word for war, *Krieg*."

"Do you know any other words from the war?"

"Well, your grandfather had a friend who claimed the army served a dark-brown drink called *cofftea*, but I think that was a word he made up himself. I once asked your great-aunt Lenore what expressions she remembered—she was an army nurse. She said she remembered only one word, and that was Spam!"

"They had the Internet back then?" I asked.

"Certainly not," she exclaimed, shaking her head. "But actually, I don't know how Spam turned into a computer word. Why don't you look that up for your project?"

Oops, parental advice again. "Bye, Mom. Gotta get to work."

"Hi, guys," I said, when the computer was turned on and Edmund and Lexie appeared. "I need to look up war words. What about this spam business? And what other kinds of words have come out of wars? I don't get it. Who is going to spend their time coming up with new words, or even funny words, with all the awful stuff that goes on in wars?"

Krieg and blitz

Kriegie or *kriegy* was short for *Kriegsgefengener,* or prisoner of war. The word *Krieg* was also a root word of *Blitzkrieg*—literally, the "lightning war" by which Germany overran much of Europe in 1940–41. *Blitz* became the common term for the 1941 bombing raids on London, and a blitzkrieg eventually came to mean any onslaught. To blitz through something means to rush through or make a heavy attack (especially in football). *Blitzed* is also an adjective meaning really drunk (presumably in the sense of "bombed.")

"Actually," Edmund replied as he scrolled, "wartime life combines scary and dangerous action with boring time spent waiting around and doing camp chores. Nothing like boredom to make you think up new words. There's a selection of them right here."

Wartime Slang

During both world wars of the 20th century, new words were added to the English language, drawn from other English-speaking countries and from European and Asian states where the fighting took place.

During the Second World War, members of the air forces had more opportunities than army or navy personnel to interact with their counterparts from other countries. As a result, they exchanged more trendy slang. For instance, members of Britain's Royal Air Force adopted *What's cookin'?* from the American pilots. American pilots picked up *browned off* and *cheesed off* from the British.

Two common elements of war slang were complaints about the food and sly teasing of the people in charge. British members of the armed forces might refer to the *brass* or the *red flannel* (from the red details on an officer's uniform) or call an officer *Gussie* (from Augustus, supposedly a typical name for an officer from the British upper class). Officers' gold braid was referred to as *scrambled eggs* or sometimes *marmalade.* In World War I, American soldiers referred to the regimental sergeant-major as the *big bow-wow.* The *poodle palace* was the commanding officers' headquarters in World War II. The navy regulars took turns keeping watch, so an *admiral's watch* meant a good night's sleep.

Tommies and doughboys

The British term for a regular army man was a *Tommy*—taken from the sample recruiting papers, where the name Thomas Atkins (a British "John Doe") appeared in the space for name. The term *doughboys* for American infantrymen was used well before WWI, but there are conflicting theories about where it came from. Doughboy was eventually replaced by *G.I.* (General Infantry) in WWII and *grunt* in the Vietnam War.

Boffin

A curious word developed by the *flyboys,* that is, the air force crews, was *boffin.* Its origin is unknown, but it means a civilian scientist. It is still British and Australian slang for scientists or technical experts today. A newspaper headline might read, "Boffins discover new species."

Army chicken: wieners and beans
Bags of mystery: sausages
Blankets: pancakes
Bullets: peas
Bunny's meat: all green vegetables
Deep-sea beef: haddock
Goldfish: tinned salmon
Sharks: tinned sardines

Wartime Food

Between the food rationing that both civilians and armed forces members endured in World Wars I and II, and the relative monotony of camp food, it is not surprising that many uncomplimentary words for food emerged in wartime. Here are a few from WWII:

"Poodle palace"

Hot drinks had a bad reputation, to judge from the slang words for them. Coffee in WWII was *battery acid,* which might be mixed with *galvanized Guernsey,* or tinned milk, while British sailors drank *tonsil varnish* (cheap mess-deck tea).

◄ ► **War and peace**

The word *conchie* came out of World War I and was short for conscientious objector (someone who refused to enlist, believing the war was morally wrong). Modeled on *beatnik, peacenik* started being used in the 1960s for a pacifist or an anti-war demonstrator. Like beatniks, peaceniks were seen as unconventional and outside mainstream political opinion. The same is true of *freezeniks* (those who wanted a freeze in the development of nuclear weapons) and *draftniks* (people who opposed the U.S. draft—or compulsory enlistment—for the Vietnam War). Peaceniks were also called *doves,* from the bird that is the symbol of peace, while those who were seen as more willing to go to war were *hawks.*

"Talking of food," said Lexie, "brings us to Spam. Here's how a canned meat gave us a computer term."

"Doves and hawks"

Spam

Spam, the name for the canned spiced-ham mixture created by Hormel Foods in the U.S., became an important part of the language in WWII. Since it did not require refrigeration, Spam was a regular item in both military and civilian diets. Millions of cans were sent to the Soviet Union, to Britain, and to prisoners of war. Nikita Khrushchev, the postwar Soviet leader, claimed that Spam was responsible for helping his country make it through the war. Because it appeared so regularly on their dinner plates, soldiers adopted *spam* as a term for other features of wartime life. For example, *spam medals* were those issued to almost everybody, as if they were handed out with the food rations.

Spam was ever present in the lives of kids brought up in Britain during and immediately after World War II. So when the cast of the British 1970s comedy group, Monty Python's Flying Circus, came up with a skit about a restaurant that served just one food in an unending variety of forms, it was not surprising that they chose Spam. Many computer programmers working in the 1970s were Monty Python fans. They started using the term spam for material that kept appearing when not wanted. By the time the Internet brought spam to everyone's e-mail in-box, the word was here to stay.

"Spam medals"

We've done a lot of funny words," I said, having now figured out the connection between meat and e-mail. "But there are all the bad parts of war. What about those?"

"There were many slang words for weapons, and for getting captured or killed," responded Edmund. "Even the word *blockbuster* comes from wartime; it originally meant a heavy aerial bomb; now it's something of great power or size, especially a hit movie or book. People used slang to cover up the realities of war or to help them cope with terrible situations. For instance, being in the thick of the fighting was called going to *the show,* and heading into battle was going *over the top.* A medal was a *gong.* A chestful of medals was a *fruit salad.*"

"A bayonet was a *cheese toaster,*" Lexie added, sounding a little more serious herself. "An *egg* meant a shell or bomb, and a *coffee grinder* was a machine gun. The word *pineapple* was commonly used for grenade. Sometimes a word could have both a serious and a comic meaning. In WWII American slang, *the great unknown* could mean either death or meat loaf, depending on the context. But wartime added some new words to our speech as well. Read this," she said, pointing.

Jeeps and Gremlins

The wars of the 20th century produced words that have remained in our vocabulary and aren't considered slang anymore. These include *grouse* (to complain) and *scrounge* (to acquire items by any means possible), both of which came out of the first World War. Here are some more examples.

Tank: a code word for a new type of vehicle brought into use in 1916 (so-called because the vehicles looked like cisterns, or water tanks, while they were being manufactured)

Camouflage: a French slang word initially used for theater makeup, adopted by the British army in World War I

"Camouflage"

Bazooka: an anti-tank gun. The original bazooka was a homemade instrument created from two gas pipes and a whisky funnel by American comedian Bob Burns, a popular radio personality in the 1930s and '40s. By 1943, the word referred to anti-tank rocket throwers, and Burns's instrument faded out of most people's memories.

Gremlin: First recorded in 1932, this word's etymology is unknown. It originated in the Royal Air Force and became widely used in WWII for an unidentified source of trouble.

Jeep: Opinions on the origin of the name differ. Was it called Jeep after its initials, G.P., for general purpose vehicle? Or was it named after the Jeep, a little creature who could go anywhere, appearing first in a March 1936 *Thimble Theatre* comic strip, drawn by Popeye creator E.C. Segar?

Snorkel: This word, from the German navy slang *schnorchel,* or "nose" (related to *schnarchen,* "to snore"), started being used in 1944. The object was called that because of its resemblance to a nose and also because of the noise a swimmer makes when using it. The anglicized spelling was first recorded in 1949.

"Gremlins and jeeps. Who would have thought they came out of wars?" I mused. This kind of slang seemed more serious even though the words were still funny. "I think I'll sign off for a while just to think about all this."

"Stay cool," said Edmund quietly.

"Bye for now," said Lexie. "Peace."

Speakeasies and Gumshoes

"Keep away from bootleg hootch
When you're on a spree
Take good care of yourself
You belong to me..."

Uh oh. I came home from school to find my dad singing while he made muffins. He'll sing anything... new songs, old songs, very old songs. Sometimes my mom will even sing along with him. It's embarrassing to hear parents do stuff like that.

But I was interested in *what* he was singing. I knew this was an old song called "Button Up Your Overcoat," but I'd never thought about the words before.

"Dad, I've heard of 'bootleg,' but what is 'hootch?'"

"It's a slang word for cheap alcohol—the kind bootleggers might supply. Say, that's an interesting word for your project. Why don't we look it up?"

"Never mind, Dad." I said quickly. "I'll research it myself."

So I fetched a glass of milk and a couple of muffins hot from the oven and made my way to the study to hook up with Lexie and Edmund.

"Hey there," Edmund greeted me.

"What gives?" said Lexie.

"Hi, Edmund. Hi, Lexie," I responded. "My dad was just singing about *hootch* and *bootleg*. Way back, you showed me something about slang words that come from criminal activities. Is that what we're talking about here?"

I must have blinked for a second, because suddenly Lexie was wearing a trench coat and fedora, as was Edmund. "Think of us as the *gumshoes* of the word world, the *ops* of etymology," answered Lexie, putting on a gravelly voice. "We're tough, we're gutsy, we're *hard-boiled*."

I had to laugh at her pose and at the toothpick hanging out of her mouth. Edmund's coat didn't fit him quite so well; he looked rumpled. "You guys look like something from an old movie," I exclaimed.

"The word *gumshoe*," explained Edmund, "was coined for detectives to suggest that they wore shoes with soles made of rubber (gum) or some other material that allowed them to

"Gumshoes"

Criminal slang

Some of the older slang words for criminals, often found in classics of detective fiction, include *yeggs* (originally used for a safecracker, but eventually applied to all criminals), *roughs, plug uglies,* and *goldbrickers* (swindlers). A pickpocket is a *dip,* and someone who shoplifts is getting a *five-finger discount. Perp* is short for perpetrator, someone caught perpetrating or carrying out a crime. *Hit men, triggers,* and *hired guns* are hired killers.

A *fink* is 19th-century slang for "an unpleasant, contemptible person, especially an informer, a detective, or a strikebreaker." It also became a verb in the 20th century, meaning to inform on someone or to back out of something (as in, he *finked* out).

sneak up on criminals. *Op* is short for an operative. And you are right to mention movies. You find some great criminal slang in there—and in crime novels."

"But first, you were wondering about words for *booze*," interrupted Lexie, who had been bringing up the correct page on the Web site. "Here you go."

Rotgut and Moonshine

Words for illegally produced or cheap, poor-quality alcohol are numerous and include *bathtub gin, moonshine, giggle water, rotgut,* and *hootch.* Hootch comes from Chinook jargon, a Pacific Coast trade language that mixed up bits of Chinook, Nootka, and other aboriginal languages with English and French. It was used up and down the West Coast for nearly a hundred years by aboriginal people, traders, officials, and settlers, and it is estimated that in 1900, over 100,000 people could speak it.

The years of Prohibition, from 1920 to 1933 in the U.S., encouraged the use of many slang words for illegal alcohol. While most of Canada had a milder form of Prohibition, the laws did not prevent the manufacture of alcohol. *Bootleggers* and *rumrunners* smuggled liquor into the U.S. from Canada and other countries. Bootleg means "illicitly produced, transported, or sold." Nowadays, it is also used to describe pirated music recordings (for instance, a bootleg CD). The term comes from the mid-1800s and derives from the smugglers' practice of hiding bottles in their boots.

"Bootlegger"

That last sentence made me pause. "People shoved bottles into their boots and could still *walk*?" I asked Edmund.

"Well," he answered, "it does sound funny, but perhaps boots were bigger in those days. Anyway, by the time the folks were bootlegging during Prohibition, the liquor wasn't going into their boots; it was more often transported in boats."

"You could drink the stuff at places like these," added Lexie, pointing to the screen.

Blind Pigs and Speakeasies

Chinook jargon

Another term that comes from Chinook jargon is *high muckamuck*—the person in charge, or the *big shot;* literally, "the person with plenty of food."

Those in search of drink during Prohibition might find it at a *speakeasy.* The term has Irish roots and can be found in written records as early as 1889, referring to illegal drinking establishments. To speak "easy" was to speak quietly or softly, presumably so the police wouldn't hear.

Another term for an illegal bar was a *blind pig* or, sometimes, a *blind tiger.* One theory says that these establishments offered paying customers the chance to see an unusual animal. The customers would get a "complimentary drink" as part of the package, and often they wouldn't see any animal at all. Another theory is that the windows of such establishments were blacked out or "blind."

"There are so many slang words for illegal drugs and activities that your project could be hundreds of pages long," said Lexie.

"So," I asked, "if a country somewhere made chocolate illegal, people might start coming up with slang words for it?"

"Undoubtedly," responded Edmund. "Now let's go to the other side of the equation, words for police officers and prisons. Take a look at this page."

He scrolled down to a list that started with the word "cops."

"Flatfoot"

Cops, coppers: because they "cop" or take you

Bobbies or peelers: British terms that began soon after Sir Robert Peel founded the London police force in 1826

Bulls: shortened from bulldog, this word originates in the 1700s, when it meant a sheriff's officer

Flatfoot: a term particularly applied to an officer who walked a beat

The fuzz: American slang used in the 1920s by hoboes, criminals, and carnies

Johnny darbies: a British mangling of the French word for police, *gendarmes*

Pig: a term popularized by hippies in the 1960s, which actually originated in the 19th century

Terms for special kinds of police include *bear* or *Smokey the bear* (an American highway patrol officer who wears a hat like that of Smokey the Bear), *narc* (member of the drug squad), and *Mountie* (for a member of the Royal Canadian Mounted Police).

Besides gumshoes, another term for detectives was *shamus.* It is thought to have come from the Yiddish word *shammas,* meaning the sexton of a synagogue, but its origins may also stem from the fact that Seamus is an Irish name. During much of the late 19th and early 20th centuries in the United States, policeman was a common career for an Irish person.

Jailhouse slang

Words for prison or jail are numerous. Some examples are the *can,* the *clink,* the *cooler,* the *hoosegow* (from a Mexican word for tribunal), the *graystone college,* the *big house,* the *joint,* the *jug,* the *sneezer,* the *stir,* the *slammer,* and the *tank.* Being *sent up the river* means being sent to jail.

Just then the phone rang in the study. The call was for my brother. He didn't answer my yell, so I told his friend to call back. A little while later my brother cruised by the study door. "Someone phoned," I said. "Where were you?"

"In the can," he said.

I laughed.

"What's so funny?" he demanded, coming into the room.

"I was just reading about how *in the can* is slang for being in prison," I answered, checking the computer screen nervously to see if my brother would notice anything unusual. Edmund and Lexie were standing off to one side in their trenchcoats.

"Yeah, well, it's also slang for *in the bathroom,*" he pointed out. "For that matter, it's slang in the movie business for something that's completed—you know, 'It's in the can.' Put that in your project."

He glanced at the computer. "Nice graphics on that site," he grunted as he left the room.

You know, sometimes my brother seems almost human.

"Being sent up the river"

Globetrotting Slang

Everybody had to have a title page for their projects, and our teacher had announced that she wanted to see the pages a week before the project was due. I don't like drawing pictures, and I was trying to think of what I could do instead. I decided to consult Edmund and Lexie about it the next afternoon, when I sat down in front of the computer.

"Why don't you cover the page with slang words from top to bottom?" suggested Lexie. "They could all be in different typefaces or colors."

"That sounds good," I mused. "I wonder which words I should use, though."

"How about a list of words for nonsense?" she said. " I know tons of them. *Balderdash, bosh, drivel, humbug...*"

"Wouldn't that make the teacher think my whole project is nonsense?" I worried. "Hey, what about words for 'good,' instead?"

"An excellent idea," Edmund pronounced.

Lexie looked keen, too. "Here are some that have been used in the last hundred years," she said and began rhyming off words. "*Aces up, nobby, hunky-dory, hotsy-totsy...*"

While I scribbled down as many words as I could, Edmund kept jumping in to give us some history. "*Hotsy-totsy:* a word coined by cartoonist William de Beck in his *Barney Google* comic strip in 1925."

"*Smooth, snazzy, spiffy, sweet...*" Lexie went on.

"*Sweet* is found in 1930s slang, but it has made a comeback in recent years."

"*Swell, boss, hip to the jive, killer diller, copacetic, out of this world, wizard, peachy, cool, crazy, fantabulous, fat...*"

"Peachy, cool, sweet"

"*Fat* comes from the 1950s and is a precursor to the hip-hop term *phat*," Edmund said quickly.

"*Kicky, neat, the living end, real basic, bad, far out, nutty, solid, too much, wild, beautiful, sharp, something else, righteous,* and *wicked,*" Lexie stopped to take a deep breath while I wrote like crazy.

"Thanks, you two," I said, looking over the page I'd filled with words. "This should give me the title page of the century. A lot of this slang is American, isn't it? Do all countries develop their own slang?"

"Indeed they do," answered Edmund. "Sometimes the same word will mean two different things in two different countries. The result can be confusing or even accidentally offensive. As well, different countries like to make slang in different ways. For instance, the British and the Australians use more rhyming slang than we do in North America."

"Can you give me some examples?" I asked.

"No problemo," answered Lexie, as the screen changed. "Have a go."

Pit privies

What is known formally as a pit privy has acquired many names in different countries. North American terms include *outhouse, backhouse, biffy,* and *kybo.* In Australia, it is called a *dunny* or *longdrop* (a term also used in South Africa).

Joannas and Trouble

For centuries, rhyming slang was spoken by Cockneys, people who lived in a certain poor neighborhood of London, England. But this kind of slang gradually spread in the 19th and 20th centuries, partly through emigration and partly when men and women from different parts of Britain were thrown together in the armed forces during wartime. Now it is commonly used in British speech. Classic Cockney rhyming slang expressions include:

Joanna: piano   *Porkies (pork pies):* lies

Loaf of bread: head   *Titfer (tit for tat):* hat

Mince pies: eyes   *Trouble and strife:* wife

Plates of meat: feet

"Rhyming slang has survived in a few expressions in North America," Edmund added. "One of them is a *raspberry*. You know, a *Bronx cheer*, the sound a whoopee cushion makes."

Lexie jumped in. "It's short for *raspberry tart*, which is rhyming slang for f...."

"I can't put that in a school project!" I protested.

"I suppose not," answered Edmund. "How about 'Put up your *dukes*,' which is uttered by would-be fighters. *Dukes* is short for *Duke of Yorks*, which rhymes with forks. *Forks*, in turn, was traditional slang for fingers—and, by extension, fists."

"That I can put in," I said, as Edmund scrolled down to the section on Australian slang.

◄ | ►

Rhyming slang

Present-day Ireland and Scotland have developed rhyming slang based on their own pronunciation and references. For instance, a Scot might say, "Are you *corned beef*?" to mean "Are you deaf?" because corned beef rhymes with deaf as the Scottish pronounce it. An Irish person might say *"jimmy joyce"* (after Irish writer James Joyce) for voice.

"Raspberry"

Slang Down Under

The early British and Irish settlers in Australia were often poor and uneducated people who had emigrated in order to better themselves, or criminals who had been "transported" (shipped to Australia as punishment). They carried their slang with them, and rhyming slang is still common in Australia. "Have a look" is *Have a Captain Cook* or *Have a captain's.* (Captain Cook was one of the first Europeans to visit Australia.) Here are some other examples.

Al Capone, dog and bone: phone
Bag of fruit: a man's suit
Billy lid: kid, young child (a billy is a metal cooking pot)
Dog's eye: meat pie
Gin sling: ring, a phone call, as in "Gimme a gin on the dog"
Noah (Noah's ark): shark

Other Australian words are created by shortening words and often adding a vowel. A barbecue is a *barbie,* a work break is a *smoko,* Christmas is *Chrissie,* and university is *uni.* A *chalkie* (teacher) might take his *sangers* (sandwiches) to a picnic and look for a good *possie* (position or place) to watch the *footy* (football).

When you combine rhyming slang with word shortening and adding vowels, you come up with words like *seppo* for an American. How do you get there? American = Yank = rhymes with septic tank = shortened to seppo.

Mickey

Canadians call a half-sized bottle of alcohol a *mickey*, derived from the slang word *michael,* a hip flask, which in turn comes from the common Irish name and also the derogatory image of Irish people as being too fond of alcohol. In the U.S., a mickey is short for *Mickey Finn,* a knockout drug, but that usage is derived from the name of a saloon keeper in Chicago.

"Whew," I said. "Sometimes slang is so confusing."

Edmund nodded. "And even countries that are close together geographically can develop different slang. Canada has some words that are quite distinct from U.S. slang, as you can see." He pointed to a new section on the screen.

Slang in the Great White North

"In Canada we have enough to do keeping up with two spoken languages without trying to invent slang, so we just go right ahead and use English for literature, Scotch for sermons and American for conversation."

—Canadian humorist Stephen Leacock

Canada has English and French as its two official languages. The slang of the English-speaking citizens is often a mixture of American and British words, but there are some particularly Canadian slang words and meanings.

Double-double: a coffee with double cream and double sugar

Hoser: an idiot, a goof; an uncultivated person, especially an inarticulate, beer-drinking lout (the origin is unknown, but the word was popularized by the characters Bob and Doug McKenzie on the Canadian comedy show *SCTV*)

Keener: a person, especially a student, who is extremely eager or enthusiastic

Pogey: unemployment insurance or welfare, depending on the context. In the U.S., this word developed as a term for the poorhouse or the workhouse—in hobo slang—or for jail

Saw-off: a tie or a draw

Two-four: a case of 24 bottles of beer (known in Australia as a *slab*)

"Double-double"

"And," added Lexie, "Canada also has *poutine,* that delicious mixture of French fries, gravy, and cheese curds invented in Quebec."

"Sounds good," I said. "Hmmm, there's still a while till dinner. A cheese sandwich would taste good right now. Thanks again for that title page, guys."

"No sweat," said Lexie.

"Catch you later," Edmund added.

When my teacher saw my title page, she said, "I like this *big time!*" (Maybe *she* should be doing the project on slang.)

That evening, as I turned the computer on, I realized that the deadline for my project was less than a week away. I'd learned a lot of slang words by now, and whenever I heard or saw a new word anywhere, I began wondering if it was slang. When I called up my notes on the screen, Edmund and Lexie were there to greet me.

Slang over time

Pinch has meant to steal for hundreds of years. *Bully* was slang for good a hundred years ago. And *copacetic* meant excellent or first-rate in the 1910s. Thirty years later, it meant smooth. Ten years after that, it also had a meaning of confidential or secret. Nowadays, it means excellent once again, or working smoothly.

"Hi there," I started in. "I've got my title page. I've got my rough notes, and I've added more ideas from the stuff we've talked about. But I need to pull it all together somehow."

"Let's start by going over your points again," suggested Edmund.

"Good idea," I answered. "Here's what I've got so far."

Lexie leaned against the edge of the screen as I started reading out my points.

1. People have been using slang for thousands of years to make the language more lively.

2. Slang words can come from the names of real people or places, or they can come from books. Slang can be made by turning words around, by misspelling them, or by using rhyming words. Sometimes slang is borrowed from other languages.

3. Sometimes we can trace the origin of a word, but often we can't. A slang word can be used by people in conversation for a long time before anyone writes it down. Sometimes there are several different theories for the origin of a term.

4. People used to be snobbish about slang and think it wasn't proper to use it. Nowadays, that has changed, but there are still times when slang doesn't seem appropriate.

Snobbish about slang

5. Lots of words begin as terms from particular kinds of work. Then they go on to be more widely used.

6. Some slang words keep the same meaning for hundreds of years. Other words change their meaning frequently, even though people keep using the words.

7. Sometimes words we think are new are really old slang words that someone has started using again.

"Nailed it"

"That's great," said Lexie. "Now add in examples from all the different words we talked about, and you'll ace this."

"You're sailing," agreed Edmund. "So we're history now."

"You're leaving?" I was startled. "But I've been relying on you for help."

"You've got the picture, you've nailed this," answered Lexie. "Your project will be the real McCoy."

"But it's not just that I want the help. I'll miss you!" I exclaimed. "You've shown me all sorts of cool words, and now I know that slang can be fun."

The real McCoy

There are many explanations for the phrase *the real McCoy.* One slang dictionary gives six possibilities, four taken from real people named McCoy, one from the name of an explosive, and one as a derivation of "real Macao," a term used for a high grade of heroin.

"Well, you never know when you might see us again. There are other projects and many other words to explore," Edmund consoled me.

"You may find we have other sites up our sleeves," said Lexie, winking at me.

"Well, I hope I do see you again," I said. "But before I say good-bye—or what's that expression you used, 'au reservoir'?—I've got one more question to ask you. Many slang words come from people's jobs, right? So do teachers have their own slang?"

"Sorry, that we can't tell you," Edmund and Lexie grinned. "Good luck. It's been real."

And with a wave, both of them disappeared from the screen.

I finished up the project on my own over the next couple of days. Edmund and Lexie had shown me enough that I was able to put it all together pretty well. I was happy with the three questions I came up with for the class presentation, too.

1. Some slang words originated a long time ago, went out of fashion and then became popular again. Can you think of a word or expression you would like people to use again?

2. New slang words are used in speech long before they are written down. Can you think of some new slang words that people should be recording now?

3. *Thingamajig* is a slang word for something whose name you have temporarily forgotten. How many other words for thingamajig can you think of?

I handed my project in on the day it was due. I still missed Lexie and Edmund, and for a while I tried to get back to the Slangalicious site. I didn't have any luck. But I thought of my two computer friends whenever I saw slang in the newspaper or on TV or on ads and billboards.

I got an A on my project. The teacher thought it was "very original." When I came home and told my parents, they were pleased for me—but then they got started with the ideas again! My mom began it. "You know, a topic like that could lead you into all sorts of interesting subjects: different dialects, how words get pronounced..."

My dad cut in. "Not to mention nicknames, and where place names come from..."

"Mom, Dad," I said. "Lay off my chops. Cool your jets and let me jell."

Before they could say any more, I grabbed myself some sinkers and moo juice and split the scene.

Further Reading

Because slang changes rapidly, too much of it can make a book seem out of date. Writers often avoid using slang in novels for this reason. If you look carefully, though, you will find lots of examples of it in your reading. Slang is sometimes used to establish a historical period or, especially in older books, to characterize a mischievous character (e.g. Mark Twain's Tom Sawyer or L.M. Montgomery's Davy Keith). British and Australian books often incorporate interesting slang from those countries. The Harry Potter books, for instance, offer some good examples of British slang, such as "wheeze" (a trick), "kip" (sleep), and "barking" (absolutely crazy).

Here are a few more books you might like to read if you're interested in exploring slang.

Curtis, Christopher Paul. *Bud Not Buddy*. New York: Delacorte Press, 1999. The author uses slang brilliantly to recreate the world of African-American jazz musicians in the 1930s in this award-winning novel.

Day, Alexandra. *Frank and Ernest*. New York: Scholastic Inc., 1988.
Day, Alexandra. *Frank and Ernest Play Ball*. New York: Scholastic Inc., 1990.
Day, Alexandra. *Frank and Ernest: On the Road!* New York: Scholastic Inc., 1994.
Day's delightful picture books introduce readers of any age to the worlds of diner slang, baseball slang, and trucker slang.

Terban, Marvin. *The Scholastic Dictionary of Idioms: More than 600 Phrases, Sayings and Expressions*. New York: Scholastic Reference, 1998.
Terban includes a number of slang words in this entertaining collection of words and phrases.

Selected Sources

My research involved looking at a wide number of books on various aspects of language, as well as reading many children's books to discover how slang has been used in young people's literature over the years. A sample of sources is given below. Because the origins of so many slang terms are shrouded in history, all the words I refer to in this book were cross-checked in as many sources as possible (standard dictionaries, slang dictionaries, Web sites, and other books).

Cassell's Dictionary of Slang, edited by Jonathon Green (London: Cassell & Co., 1998) is a thorough etymological exploration of slang in many parts of the English-speaking world, including Australia and the West Indies. Another major work is *The New Dictionary of American Slang*, edited by Robert L. Chapman (New York: Harper & Row, 1986). Both are valuable not only for their listings of words but also for their scholarly introductions on the development of slang.

Flappers 2 Rappers (Springfield, Mass.: Merriam-Webster, 1996) is Tom Dalzell's thoroughly researched examination of American youth slang of the 20th century, arranged by decade and humorously illustrated. It provided not only information, but inspiration—because of its lively tone and interesting approach. Another colorful work is the amusingly named *Straight from the Fridge, Dad,* a collection of "cool" hipster slang by Max Décharné (New York: Broadway Books, 2001).

Additional information on the history of slang came from Irving Lewis Allen's *The City in Slang: New York Life and Popular Speech* (New York: Oxford University Press, 1993) and Simeon Potter's *Our Language* (Harmondsworth: Penguin Books, 1950).

In finding ways to use slang in the narrative sections of the book, I also relied on slang thesauruses, including *The Slang Thesaurus* by Jonathon Green (Harmondsworth: Penguin Books, 1986), *The Random House Thesaurus of Slang* by Esther Lewin and Albert E. Lewin (New York: Random House, 1988), and *NTC's Thematic Dictionary of American Slang* by Richard A. Spears (Lincolnwood: NTC Publishing Group, 1993).

For sports words, I relied both on Web sites focusing on specific sports and on Harvey Frommer's *Sports Roots* (New York: Atheneum, 1979) and Tim Considine's *The Language of Sport* (New York: Facts on File, 1982).

Eric Partridge's *A Dictionary of Forces Slang 1939–1945* (London: Secker & Warburg, 1948) was particularly useful in the area of wartime slang, as was Paul Dickson's excellent book *War Slang: American Fighting Words and Phrases since the Civil War* (New York: Pocketbooks, 1994).

Canadian words can be found in *A Concise Dictionary of Canadianisms* by Walter S. Avis (Toronto: Gage Educational Publishers, 1973) and in two books by Bill Casselman: *Casselman's Canadian Words* (Toronto: Little Brown & Co. (Canada), 1995) and *Casselmania* (Toronto: Little Brown & Co. (Canada), 1996). *The Canadian Oxford Dictionary* provided the appropriate source for cross-checking all words.

Three valuable Web sites that deal with word origins include many common slang words: www.etymonline.com, www.takeourword.com, and www.wordorigins.org. An online collection of slang is www.probertencyclopaedia.com/slang.htm, made up of contributions from readers around the world; as such, it is not completely reliable, but it is extensive and informative.

In addition, there are thousands of interesting sites to explore if you are looking for particular kinds of slang (from computers to mountain biking to baseball or football). Some are more authoritative than others, but one fascinating site is Carny Lingo at www.goodmagic.com/carny, which explores a wide variety of circus and carnival slang in North America and Europe.

Index